REMBRANDT AND TURNER:
Mythical Masters

Edward Lucie-Smith

Cv/Visual Arts Research Series199

**Rembrandt and Turner:
Mythical Masters**

Edward Lucie-Smith

ISBN: 9781910110133

Cv Publications www.tracksdirectory.ision.co.uk

Rembrandt and Turner:
Mythical Masters

The Rembrandt and Turner exhibitions, one at London's National Gallery, the other at Tate Britain, are populist homages to two of the undoubted giants of the European cultural tradition. They do not attempt complete surveys. Instead they seek to found themselves on a now well-established but in fact comparatively recent myth: that of a 'late style', wherein a great artist, nearing the end of his life, somehow transcends all the works he has made previously. Titian and Michelangelo have also been the subjects of the same kind of mythologisation.

The facts are, of course, that neither Rembrandt nor Turner attained a very great age by 21st century standards. The Rembrandt show covers the artist's last decade-and—half, roughly speaking from the time when he went bankrupt in 1656 to his death in October 1669, aged 63. Turner had a longer life, but the show at Tate Britain covers about the same amount of ground – from 1835, when the artist was sixty, until his death in 1851, aged 76.

The idea of the 'late style', as a very special, magical phase in the evolution of the work of a great artist, is, as I have just said, a comparatively modern invention. To the credit of the organisers, the catalogue of the Rembrandt exhibition is careful to spell this out.

As Jonathan Bikker and Gregor J.M. Weber write in an essay entitled 'Explaining Late Rembrandt': "At the beginning of the twentieth century the search for specific rules governing the evolution of styles gave rise to a mythology of the aged artistic genius, driven to produce outstanding works in the face of his approaching death." They add to this: "The concept of *'Alterstil'* (old age style) emerged to account for late-life creativity…According to the authors who coined the term, the characteristics that defined *Alterstil*… were a tendency towards abstraction and formal simplicity, combined with greater depth in the subjective and intellectual content. The assumption was that these characteristics can be identified in all art forms and eras."

With these two exhibitions, as also with the release in Britain of Mike Leigh's much lauded new film <u>Mr. Turner</u>, one is therefore dealing with a new phase in the evolution of a myth not as yet formulated in either of the two artists' own lifetimes.

The myth, endorsed by the two museums concerned as instruments of official culture, inevitably affects our own reactions to what is shown.

One of its effects is to bring the works we are looking art closer to our own contemporary sensibilities. We are certainly not seeing them in the same way as tat of the audiences to which they were originally addressed. We are, instead, being presented within a framework where they can confidently be regarded as the productions of genius. It must be immediately noted that the idea of the 'genius' – artistic, musical or literary – was itself not fully evolved until, at its earliest, the later years of the 18th century, the period of the *Sturm und Drang*. There is considerable evidence that Rembrandt's contemporaries were often puzzled, or made to feel uneasy, by the stylistic evolution that both artists underwent in the concluding phases of their respective careers. So indeed ere many of Turner's original admirers, even though the Romantic Movement was by then in full swing.

 The Rembrandt show, held in the cramped basement spaces of the National Gallery's modern extension, suffers from curatorial overkill. A good selection of paintings from Rembrandt's last fifteen years is on view, among them a number of acknowledged masterpieces, such as the *Jewish Bride* from the Rijksmuseum in Amsterdam, which may also be a marital double portrait, and the huge (though still cut down) *Conspiracy of the Batavians under Claudius Civilis* borrowed from Stockholm.

There is also an array of self-portraits, which do much to explain why Rembrandt is today regarded as an 'honorary contemporary', in a fashion denied to other major painters of the same epoch, such as Rubens. We seem to be offered direct access to the artist's innermost thoughts and feelings.

The impact of the show is nevertheless diminished by the fact that the general effect is so cluttered. The paintings are accompanied by a mass of late period drawings and prints, impossible to examine in any detail in the thronging crowd of spectators. One longs to be able to stand back and take an unobstructed look at the major items. The situation calls to mind the late Sir John Pope-Hennessey's disapproving remark: "Pictures are made to be looked at, and not to be smelled."

The *Late Turner* show at Tate Britain occupies more spacious quarters and is much more logically hung. The artist's magically vaporous late landscape paintings have long been revered as the very pinnacle of British achievement in the visual arts, and it is an enormous pleasure to see them so generously presented. The catalogue leaves one no doubt, however, about the negative reactions of many of the artist's contemporaries. His two Venetian scenes dated 1846, *Going to the Ball* and *Returning from the Ball,* were exhibited more or less pre-sold at the Royal Academy - Turner was of course a member, an Academician in the strict sense of that term. Yet the buyers pulled out, after unfavorable reactions in the press. The painting remain unsold, and formed part of the artist's estate when he died.

Turner emerges not merely as a visionary, but as someone who had a sophisticated awareness of the processes of change in the Britain of the first half of the 19th century. The celebrated *Rain, Steam and Speed – The Great Western Railway* (1844) is a good example. The catalogue note on the painting appositely remarks that: "Nature's sublimity is controlled and condensed by the new industrial paradigm, when water is transformed by heat to produce motive power."

Nevertheless, as the exhibition is at some pains to establish, Turner's art also had deep roots in the classic landscape painting of the past, in particular in the work of Claude and Poussin. There are frequent references to mythological themes, and to be fully understood what he did often needs to be seen within the intellectual framework of an old-fashioned classical education. If Turner does at moments emerge as being, in some respects at least, the prophet of the great changes that the Industrial Revolution was going to bring about in British, and indeed the whole of European society, one cannot say that this is the be-all and end-all of his work. His fascination with Venice, then as now the least industrial or urban landscapes, is enough to certify that.

It makes even less sense to try to force Rembrandt's work into moulds that would not have been understood by his contemporaries, nor indeed, one suspects, by the artist himself. There are three strands intertwined in Rembrandt's work that make him an important forerunner of the kind of society and the kind of sensibility we have now, and this is certainly good reason why his work continues to engage audiences in a way denied to many of the artists, some of them undoubtedly major figures, who were his contemporaries. All of these strands are duly represented in the National Gallery exhibition.

There is, first, the bourgeois/capitalist background. Rembrandt, the son of a miller, did not have princes and aristocrats for patrons. Secondly, there is the influence of Protestantism. Rembrandt's treatment of the narratives he found in the Bible is always very direct. For him, as for all Protestants, the relationship with the sacred texts was unmediated by the diktats of any long-established religious hierarchy. Thirdly, also rooted in Protestantism, there is the search for the true self, which we find in his powerful self-portraits. There are glimpses of this search in the productions of earlier artists – good instances are Dürer's self-portrait, where he presents himself as a kind of surrogate for Christ, and Michelangelo's self-portrait in the Sistine Chapel, where he offers his own likeness on the flayed skin held by St Bartholomew. There are also the self-portraits offered by major Baroque artists of Rembrandt's own generation – Rubens, Van Dyck, Velasquez. None of these, however, explored the theme in such a variety of moods. One has to wait until the 19th century for artists who pursue it with a similar assiduity.

These self-portraits have played a large part in establishing Rembrandt, with professional commentators and also with the general public, as a creator who leaps out of time, who speaks to us in the here-and-now, as one of our own contemporaries.

Contributors to the National Gallery's Rembrandt catalogue would like to link the loose 'experimental' technique of the late paintings to this process of self-realisation, and to link that, in turn, to the psychology of old age. Yet they also cannot resist trying to link it to something else – to the concept of *sprezzatura* put forward by Castiglione in *The Courtier*. Castiglione defines this quality as follows: "A certain nonchalance, so as to conceal all art and make whatever one does or says appear to be without effort and almost without any thought about it."

They link this, in turn, to Vasari's praise of Titian, as paraphrased by the Dutch author Carel van Mander. Titian, van Mander said, produced work "painted with great art, but [which] conceals the labour." And they go on to quote some verses about 'An Old Man's Head, by Rembrandt', written by the minor English poet John Elsum, and first published in 1700:

> What a coarse rugged Way of Painting's here,
> Stroaks upon Stroaks, Dabbs upon Dabbs appear.
> The Work you'd think was huddled up in haste,
> But mark how truly ev'ry Colour's plac'd,
> With such Oeconomy in such a sort,

That they each mutually support.
Rembrandt! They Pencil plays a subtil Part
This Roughness is contriv'd to hide the Art.

This is all very well, until you actually start to make comparisons between Titian's late paintings and those of Rembrandt. Emotionally they seem to be worlds apart from one another. If there is one thing late Rembrandt is not, it is in any sense elegant. The nearest he ever gets to it is in the celebrated portrait of *Jan Six*, illustrated in the catalogue but not in the NG version of the show. One is tempted to cite the old cliché: "One swallow doesn't make a summer."

The difference between late Titian and late Rembrandt is especially conspicuous if you compare their respective treatments of the female nude. Titian's late nudes remain mythological creatures: embodiments, despite certain Mannerist eccentricities, of the classical ideal. Rembrandt's nudes are naked women, no more and no less.

When Rembrandt does tackle classical themes – an image of June, two versions of Lucretia doing away with herself – it is remarkable how deliberately 'un-classical' his treatment of them is. His *Juno*, from the Hammer Museum in Los Angeles, is a sumptuously dressed matron, a step up from the matrons of the Amsterdam *haute bourgeoise* thanks chiefly to her magnificent necklace and coronet. She's grasping a staff and is very ready to tell you what to do, but she doesn't look as if she has just stepped down from Olympus. Instead she looks as if she's interviewing you for a job in the servants' quarters of the town mansion her new-rich husband has just built for her.

In fact what most strikes me about the later phase of Rembrandt's work is not a sense of an artist ripening into wisdom, nor of a kind of supreme technical fluency (the less-is-more attitude summed up in the Italian word *sprezzatura*), but its essential modernist in some respects, and its distance from our own attitudes to art in others.. As the record shows, Rembrandt was, in his latter years, working under intense economic pressure. Partly this was due to his lack of financial judgment. He had over-expanded, over-spent and bankrupted himself. Before this downfall he seems to have run an operation that was at least in some respects comparable to the way that fashionable artists, such as Jeff Koons and Damien Hirst operate today. The continuing controversies about what is really Rembrandt and what is just the boutique version – products of the studio, but not from the master's own hand – bear witness to this. Modern experts tend to over-idealise the great masters whose work they have fallen in love with. Homer is never allowed to nod. When there's no standard of 'finish' against which to measure a given work, these quarrels tend to intensify. The celebrated <u>Polish Rider</u> in the Frick Collection in New York (illustrated in the catalogue but not included in the NG show) is a case in point. World famous, then not too long ago rejected from Rembrandt's *oeuvre* by a number of supposedly well-qualified experts, it is now back in favour.

In addition, no artist whatever his degree of success at some period in his own lifetime, can count on remaining steadfastly at the top. The reputations of some – one thinks of various once-grand Victorian academic artists – are swiftly eclipsed after their deaths. Others unexpectedly fall from grace in mid-career.

Another famous Rembrandt painting, *The Conspiracy of the Batavians under Claudius Civilis*, which is indeed present in the exhibition, supplies an instructive case. Reluctantly commissioned for the decoration of Amsterdam Town Hall (after Govert Flinck, who was to have supplied all the huge paintings required, inconveniently died of plague), Rembrandt's canvas occupied the space allotted to it for a very brief time indeed – just a few months in 1662. It re-appeared in an anonymous auction held in Amsterdam in 1734, and made its way to Sweden before 1667.

By that time the painting had been considerably cut down. What now remains is just the centre of the composition. Various reasons have been offered as to why the work met with no favour. One is the somewhat brutal representation of the central figure, who, like the Nordic God Odin, had lost an eye. Essentially what seems to have happened was that Rembrandt was being pushed aside by a younger generation of artists, some of whom – such as Flinck – had been his pupils. This changing of the guard is a not unfamiliar phenomenon in the history of art. Today in Britain the YBAs (Younger British Artists), who made such a stir in the 1990s, are being cast into the shade by newer talents. Their resounding triumph, at the Royal Academy's *Sensation!* show of 1997, is already half-forgotten.

A lesson of the NG exhibition is the degree to which Rembrandt responded to specific types of patronage, generated within the society of his time (in many respects unlike ours) and specifically linked to the mercantile urban community of which he formed a part. The Dutch republic had no aristocracy, and the Town Hall commissions were a rate example of public, governmental patronage. Some of his more ambitious paintings, both during this late period, and before it, were group portraits, representing various sorts of collective association or activity. An example in the NG show is the work popularly known as *The Syndics,* painted in 1662. The full title is *The Sampling Officials of the Amsterdam Drapers' Guild.* It shows a group of men who were charged with monitoring the quality of the dyed woollen cloth produced in Amsterdam, and originally hung in the headquarters of the city's Draper's Guild. Frans Hals produced group portraits of the same type, working not in Amsterdam but in Haarlem. A comparable example is *The Governors of the Old Men's Almshouse at*

Haarlem. This, dated 1664, is just as loose in technique as the painting by Rembrandt.

Things worth noting in this context are, first, the fact that Rembrandt depended heavily on the demand for portraits, in order to make a living, and second, that his sitters tended to be middle aged or older – the exceptions being when he was commissioned to produce a family group. Images of children or young people seen on their own tend to represented members of his own family, most notably his son Titus. No doubt it was older people who had enough money to consider having likenesses made.

Rembrandt's portraits, when compared with those produced by Flemish artists of the same epoch, such as Rubens and Van Dyck, are notable for their sobriety – even, one might say, for their general air of melancholy. The sitters in contemporary portraits by Hals wear clothing that is equally restrained but are generally much more cheerful in demeanor. One has to ask oneself if this was something that Rembrandt imposed on his sitters or if it was, in general, a mood that they found for themselves, as products of a notably sober, God-fearing society. Hals may, perhaps, have been a more sociable being. The ageing Rembrandt seems to have lived within a very small circle.

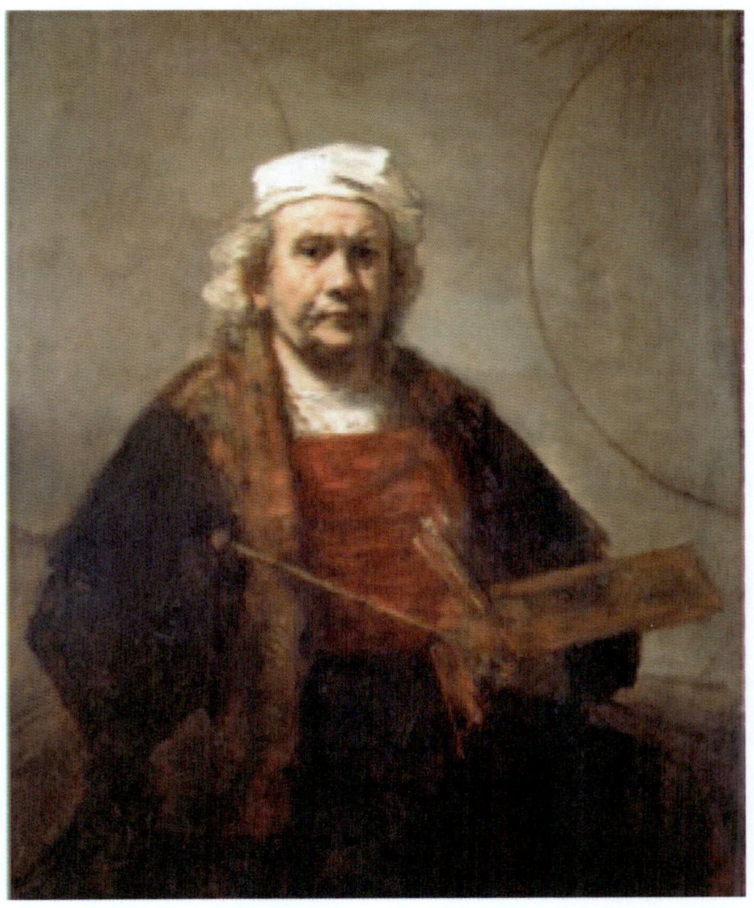

Rembrandt Self Portrait with Two Circles about 1665-9 Kenwood House, The
Iveagh Bequest, English Heritage, London

The word 'God-fearing' also raises the question of Rembrandt's output of religious pictures during these final years. The subjects are drawn from the Old Testament just as frequently as they are from the New, and most refer directly to the Bible. There are few images of saints, though these include a *Self Portrait of the Apostle Paul*, and two paintings of *St Bartholomew*, one dated 1657 and the other 1661. The second of these, now in the Getty Museum, is so portrait-like you might easily mistake the intended subject – that is, if you happen to miss the knife, shown in shadow in the bottom left-hand corner, which is clasped in the saint's hand.

None of these paintings with subjects taken from the Bible were intended for display in churches, and some such as the nude *Bathsheba*, painted in 1654 and included in the NG exhibition, would have been entirely unsuitable for such a purpose. They were intended as adornments for wealthy homes and as objects for private contemplation. This is even more exactly the case with Rembrandt's numerous religious prints, intended for a wider, less affluent audience.

In producing these, Rembrandt was following in the footsteps of Dürer, who once complained that he made more money from his prints than he did from his paintings.

The birth of the religious Reformation – i.e. Protestantism – is of course closely connected to the early history of the printing press in Europe.

It is interesting that Hals, even more prolific than Rembrandt as a portraitist, never tackled themes of this kind, though he did paint some 'low-life' subjects, of a sort that sometimes appear, on a much smaller scale, in Rembrandt's prints. Hals, however, was never a print-maker.

The comparison prompts some reflections on the difference between Hals' reputation and that of Rembrandt. Hals was a generation or more older than Rembrandt, born in 1582 or 1583, whereas Rembrandt was born in 1606. He lived much longer than Rembrandt, dying in August 1666, just three years before his great contemporary. In Hals' later work the painterly technique becomes much looser – one might argue that the brushwork there is consistently freer and more fluent than that of late Rembrandt, and better deserves to be classified as a painterly equivalent of Castiglione's *sprezzatura*. Rembrandt, in his later years, often piles the paint on thick. Hals doesn't do that.

bYet Hals is never mentioned in solemn discussions of the existence of an *Alterstil*, as a defining characteristic of the work of a few very great artists. One good reason is that it is pretty well impossible to find any 'spiritual' or 'transcendental' element in his art, whether this be early in his development or late.

The fact is that theorisations about a 'late style' in art tend to remove Rembrandt from his true context. His work belongs, for all its evident greatness, to a very particular social setting – that of the Dutch 17th century. It also belongs to a period in art when the technique of oil-painting, and what was acceptable to patrons in a fully finished painting, was rapidly evolving. We see the new looseness of handling not only in Rembrandt and Hals, but also in Velasquez and Murillo, and in Italian artists of the same epoch such as Salvator Rosa and G.B. Castiglione. It was to develop further in the work of Rococo painters such as Watteau and Fragonard and would reach a culmination in the 19th century in artists otherwise as different from one another as Manet, Renoir and Cézanne. The National Gallery 'Late Rembrandt' show is in fact a work of strenuous mythologisation, designed to make us feel that this great figure from the past is indeed 'one of us'.

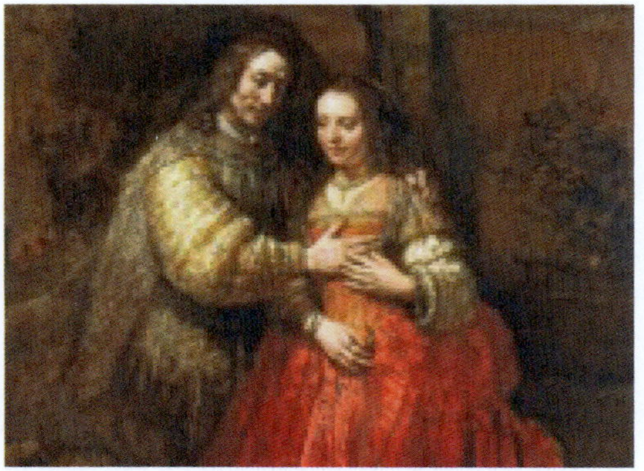

mbrandt Portrait of a Couple as Isaac and Rebecca, known as 'The Jewish Bride' about 1665 Rijksmuseum, on loan from the City of Amsterdam (A. van der Hoop Bequest) The National Gallery London

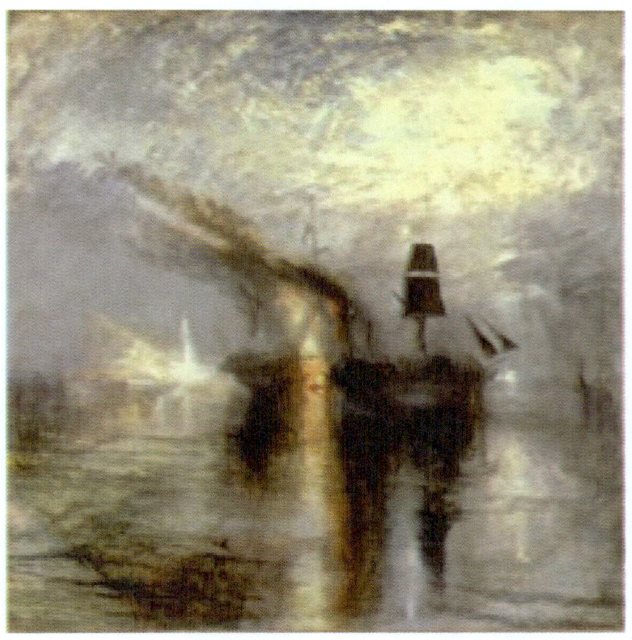

JMW Turner, *Peace - Burial at Sea* 1842 Tate. Accepted by the nation as part of the Turner Bequest 1856

The situation with Turner is only slightly different. The exhibition begins its trajectory in 1835, that is to say two decades after the end of the Napoleonic Wars. He entered the Royal Academy schools in 1789, aged only fourteen. Precociously talented, he exhibited a watercolour at the Academy's annual exhibition the very next year. He first showed an oil painting there in 1796. In 1802 he took advantage of the brief Peace of Amiens to travel to France and Switzerland.

In France, he visited Paris and studied at the Louvre. He was, long before the end of the wars, deeply versed in the work of the great masters of the European landscape tradition. Inspired by Claude's *Liber Veritatis*, he became a printmaker, and between 1806 and 1819 produced a book of prints, the *Liber Studiorum*, designed to popularise his ideas about landscape. He categorised the genre into six types: Marine, Mountainous, Pastoral, Architectural, and Elevated or Epic Pastoral. These classifications showed his keen awareness of what landscape painters had produced in the past. He also essayed a version of history painting, linked to landscape. A well-known example is *Hannibal Crossing the Alps* (1812).

Once the wars were over, Turner, who had always travelled widely within England, undertook wider travels on the Continent than he had been able to make heretofore. In search of subject matter, he went as far as Denmark and Bohemia. As the Tate Britain catalogue of the *Late Turner* show remarks: "As an artist-tourist Turner was able to share and anticipate the interests of a wider travelling public caught up in the growing boom for middle-class tourism, and eager for pictures prints and guidebooks."

Middle-class much of his public may have been, but by this time Turner was one of the most celebrated of British artists, and his celebrity gradually spread beyond Britain. In 1838, for example, he was presented with a gold snuffbox by King Louis-

Philippe of France. In 1845, he dined with the French king at Château d'Eu.

The main current within Turner's art was Romanticism, but he used existing templates to help him to express the powerful onrush of Romantic emotion. Sometimes, in his later years, he ventured somewhat beyond the comprehension of his patrons. Examples of this included in the Tate Britain exhibition are two paintings from the Turner Bequest, *Going to the Ball (San Martino)* and *Returning from the Ball (St Martha)*. Commissioned in advance by a couple of patrons, these were shown at the Royal Academy in 1845, but attracted so much criticism in the press that the intending buyers concerned pulled out. They remained unsold to form part of Turner's estate on his death.

Turner's late output is uneven. It's hard to fall in love with some of the late square format pictures. *Bacchus and Ariadne,* the first of this series, exhibited at the Royal Academy in 1840, tries to paraphrase Titian, while throwing in aspects of Claude. A contemporary critic cruelly described it as "a palette set with an omelette." The strange *The Exile and the Rock Limpet* (1842), showing the Emperor Napoleon standing on the edge of the sea, with his back to a blazing sunset, was apparently intended to be a coded rebuke to a bumptious but less successful fellow artist, Benjamin Robert Haydon. The Tate catalogue mischievously informs one that "In *Punch* in 1846, the caricaturist

Richard Doyle published a spoof of a letter from Turner describing 'my "Rock Limpet" picture – a noble work, but not understood."

Some of Turner's late paintings, chief among them the famous *Rain, Steam and Speed*, show the artist trying to come to terms with new aspects of the world he lived on, things that no landscape before him could have seen. Others, on the contrary, show him trying to renew long-established formulae. Others still, such as *The Angel in the Sun* (exhibited at the Royal Academy in 1846) show him setting foot in realms we associate both with William Blake and – less flatteringly perhaps – with the territory occupied with his slightly younger contemporary John 'Mad' Martin (1789-1854).

It is also worth remembering that *The Angel in the Sun* coincides in date with the great religious revival that was taking place in Britain at that time - a reaction against the rationalist Enlightenment ideas that had played so large a part in bringing about the French Revolution and everything that followed it. That phase of 19th century cultural history can seem very alien to us today.

What the Tate's survey of Turner's final years seems to demonstrate is that we have here an artist of genius struggling, often very successfully but sometimes not, with the demands of a rapidly changing world. It was, nevertheless, very different from the artistic world we inhabit ourselves. As Turner's work very amply demonstrates, he was, despite his reputation for being personally uncouth, he had a sophisticated knowledge and appreciation of what great landscape and seascape painters had done in the past. The famous *Bridgewater Sea-Piece*, commissioned by the first Duke of Bridgewater in 1801 as a pendant to a painting by Willem van de Velde the Younger, is enough to prove this. It skillfully echoes its model, but also extends Van de Velde's range of effects.

It is not clear, however, that Turner went on to develop what early 20th century scholars tried to define as an *Alterstil*. He is not, in his last period, consistent enough for that.

If we look at the history of Turner studies, in the period since his death, we find a consistent effort to bring him into line with what seemed to be avant-garde at the time. This is particularly true of 20th century studies of his work. First Impressionism, then the more painterly aspects of early Modernist abstract painting, then Abstract Expressionism were regarded as things he had anticipated in this late work. The paradox is this: that supporters of the new have nevertheless been anxious to justify their choices by looking for great, if isolated, exemplars in the art of the past. It is far from clear that Turner's objectives were the same as those of the artistic grandchildren and great-grandchildren whose existence has been foisted upon him.

In fact, there has recently been somewhat of a turnaround in studies of the work of the two great giants of British landscape painting – Turner and Constable. A major survey of Constable's work is on view at the Victoria & Albert Museum as I write this. The title is *Constable: The Making of a Master*, and, as the museum states: "The exhibition presents Constable's work for the first time alongside the old masters of classical landscape whose compositional ideas and formal values he revered." It would be quite possible to present an exhibition organised on exactly the same lines about Turner, demonstrating that his work has deep roots in the history of European painting, stretching back to the mid-17th century. This would perhaps be more genuinely instructive that the current show at Tate Britain, but it wouldn't nearly as easy to publicise.

Great public museums, such the National Gallery here in London and Tate Britain, are often, thanks to the kind of society we now have, held in the grip of two self-contradictory sets of ideas. First, the need to be populist – to present a mass audience with a big romantic idea that will seize the popular imagination, and bring the visitors flocking. The concept of an *Alterstil*, a sea-change that transforms the work of great artists if they have the luck to live long enough, is just such a notion. It's seductive, but the closer you look, the less convincing it becomes.

Secondly, there is the curators' wish to show that they've really done their research. The Rembrandt show, jammed into quarters which are really too small for it in its present form, and with not enough paintings available to leaven the mass of drawings and prints, is a striking, though obviously unintended, example of 'more is less'. I longed to be able to stand back, and let the paintings make there full effect. Even though that effect may not have been exactly the one the organisers intended. It's still a privilege to stand in the presence of one of Rembrandt's self-portraits. These do indeed feel completely modern.

Edward Lucie-Smith
London December 2014

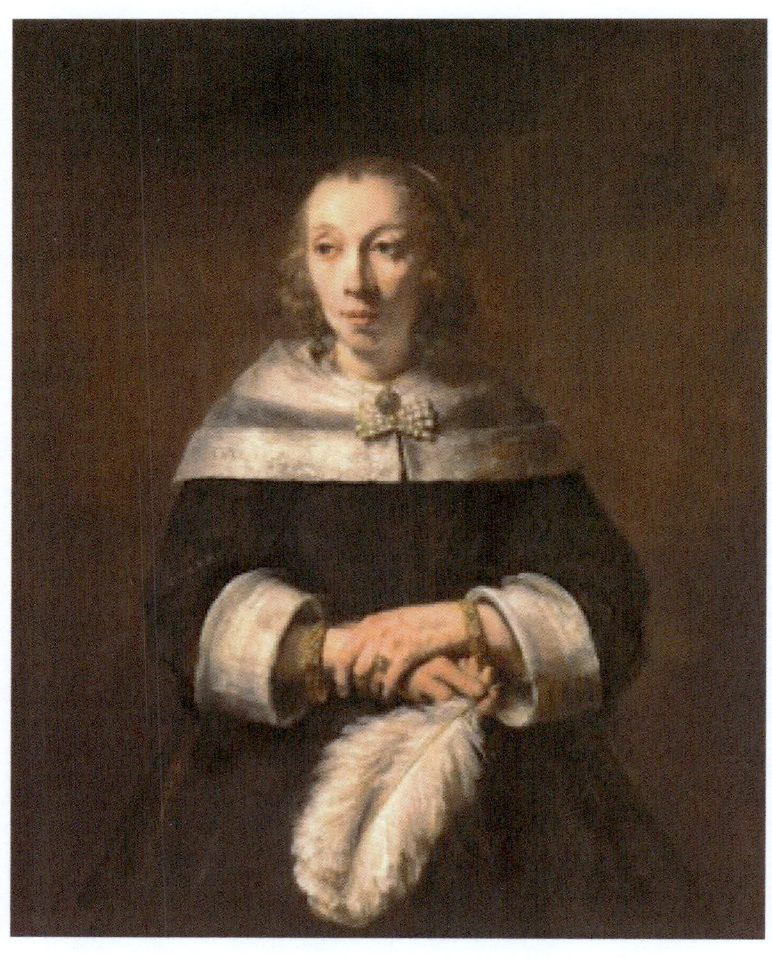

Rembrandt Portrait of a Lady with an Ostrich-Feather Fan 1658-6
National Gallery of Art, Washington, Widener Collection

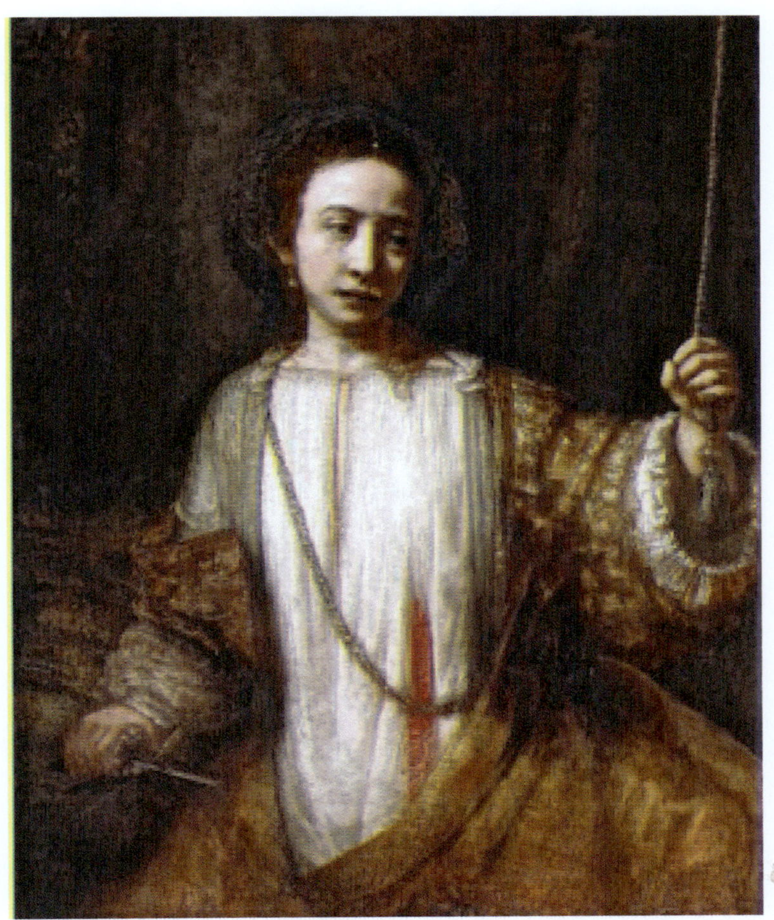

Rembrandt The Suicide of Lucretia 1666
The Minneapolis Institute of Arts, USA

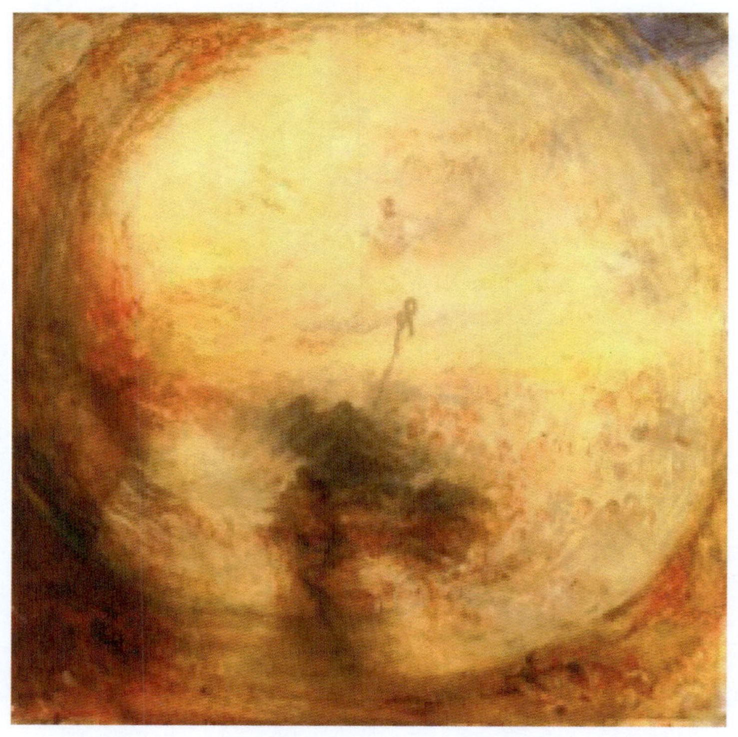

JMW Turner, Light and Colour (Goethe's Theory) - the Morning after the
Deluge - Moses Writing the Book of Genesis 1843 Tate. Accepted by the
nation as part of the Turner Bequest 1856

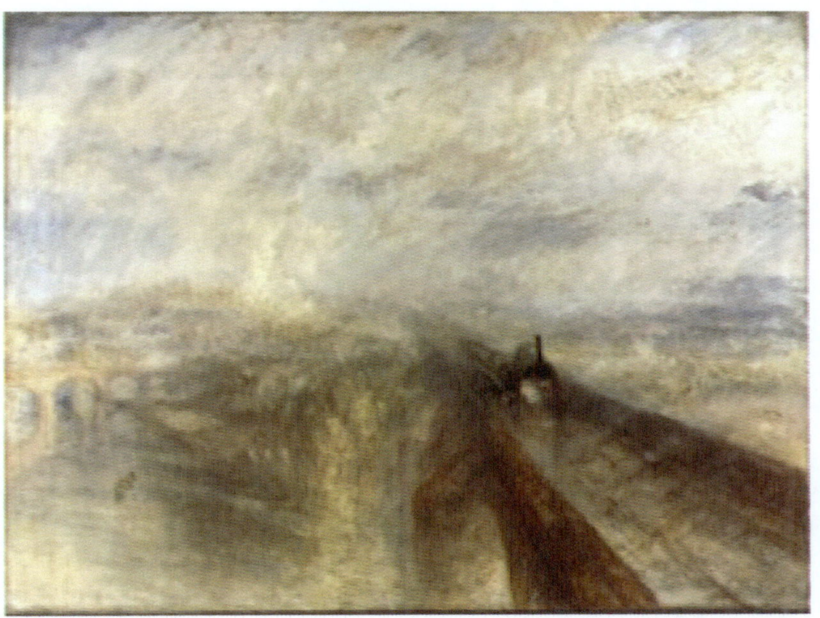

J.M.W. Turner, Rain, Steam, and Speed – The Great Western Railway 1844
Copyright The National Gallery, London

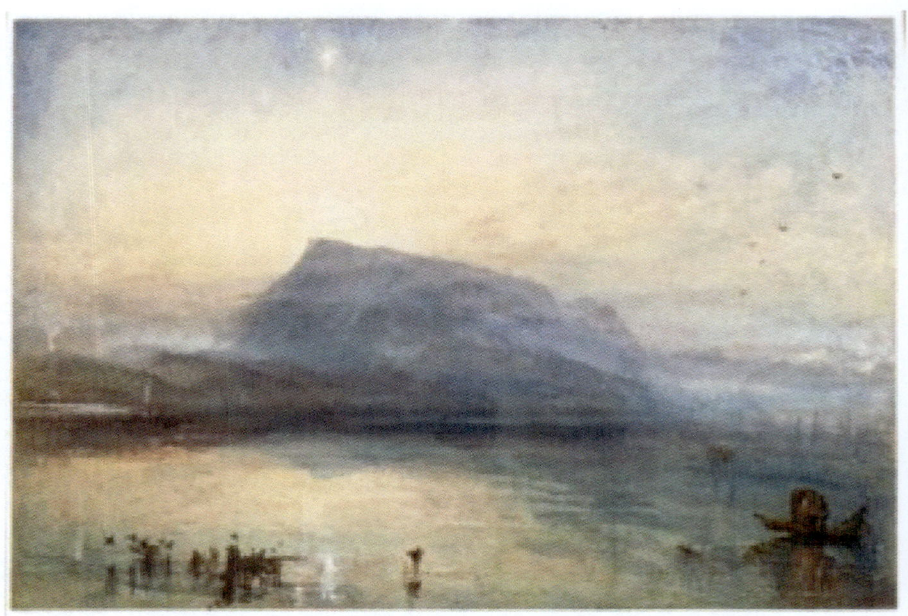

JMW Turner, Th *The Blue Rigi* 1841-2
Tate. Purchased with assistance from the National Heritage Memorial Fund, the Art
Fund (with a contribution from the Wolfson Foundation and including generous
support from David and Susan Gradel, and from other members of the public
through the Save the Blue Rigi appeal) Tate Members and other donors 2007

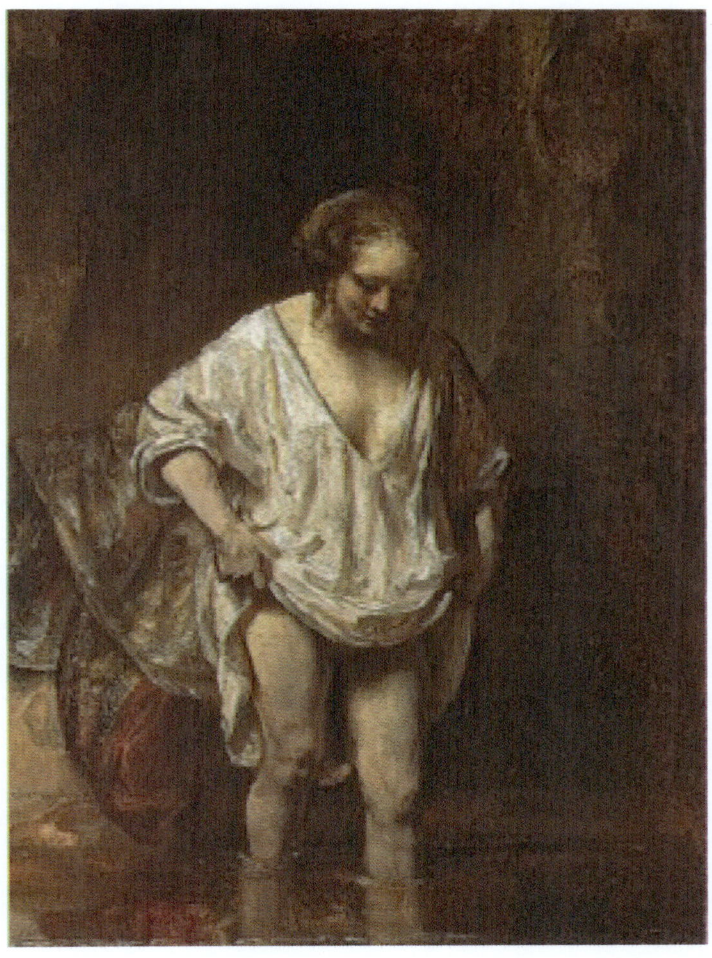

Rembrandt A Woman bathing in a Stream (Hendrickje Stoffels?)
The National Gallery, London

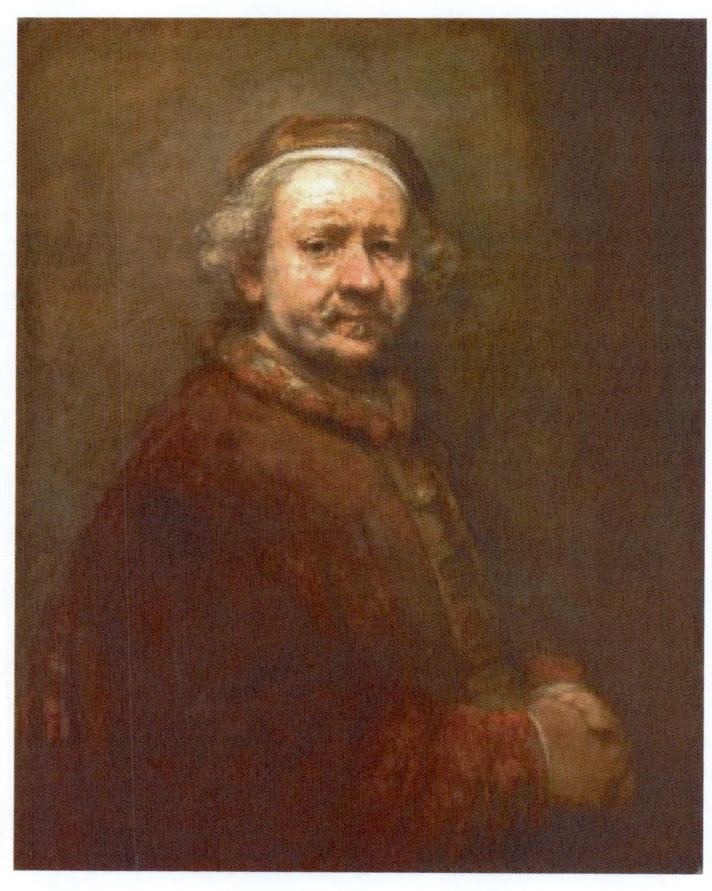

Rembrandt Self Portrait at the Age of 63 1669
The National Gallery, London

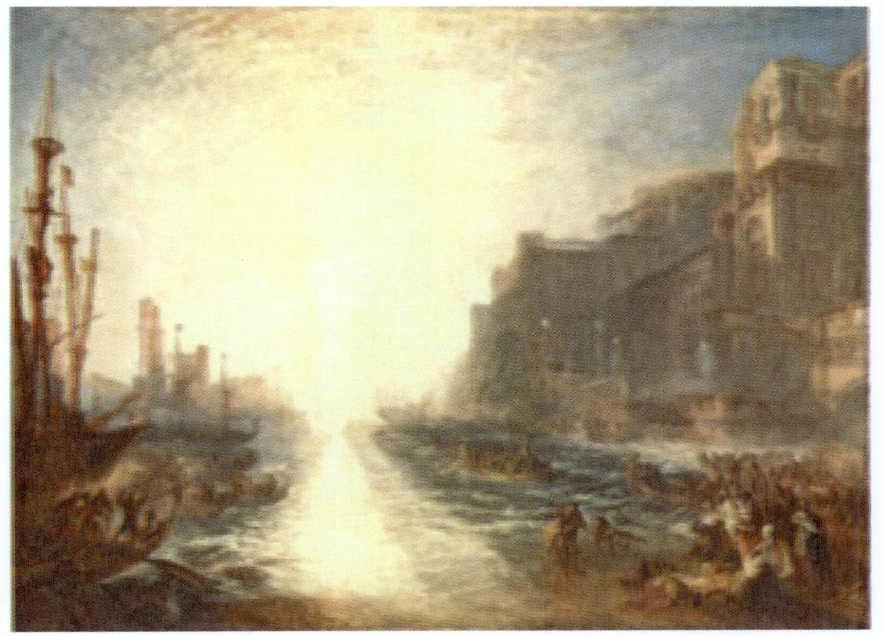

JMW Turner, *Regulus* 1837
Tate. Accepted by the nation as part of the Turner Bequest 1856

The Artists

Rembrandt was born in Leiden on July 15, 1606 - his full name Rembrandt Harmenszoon van Rijn. He was the son of a miller. Despite the fact that he came from a family of relatively modest means, his parents took great care with his education. Rembrandt began his studies at the Latin School, and at the age of 14 he was enrolled at the University of Leiden. The program did not interest him, and he soon left to study art - first with a local master, Jacob van Swanenburch, and then, in Amsterdam, with Pieter Lastman, known for his historical paintings. After six months, having mastered everything he had been taught, Rembrandt returned to Leiden, where he was soon so highly regarded that although barely 22 years old, he took his first pupils. One of his students was the famous artist Gerrit Dou.

Rembrandt moved to Amsterdam in 1631; his marriage in 1634 to Saskia van Uylenburgh, the cousin of a successful art dealer, enhanced his career, bringing him in contact with wealthy patrons who eagerly commissioned portraits. An exceptionally fine example from this period is the Portrait of Nicolaes Ruts (1631, Frick Collection, New York City). In addition, Rembrandt's mythological and religious works were much in demand, and he painted numerous dramatic masterpieces such as The Blinding of Samson (1636, Städelsches Kunstinstitut, Frankfurt). Because of his renown as a teacher, his studio was filled with pupils, some of whom (such as Carel Fabritius) were already trained artists. In the 20th century, scholars have reattributed a number of his paintings to his associates; attributing and identifying Rembrandt's works is an active area of art scholarship.

Rembrandt produced many of his works in this fashionable town house in Amsterdam (above left). Purchased by the artist in 1639, when he was 33, it proved to be the scene of personal tragedy: his wife and three of his children died here. The house became a financial burden, and in 1660 Rembrandt was forced to move. A new owner added the upper story and roof, giving it the appearance it still bears. In 1911 the Dutch movement made it a Rembrandt museum -preserving it both as a shrine of a revered national artist and as an imposing example of 17th Century Dutch architecture.

In contrast to his successful public career, however, Rembrandt's family life was marked by misfortune. Between 1635 and 1641 Saskia gave birth to four children, but only the last, Titus, survived; her own death came in 1642- at the age of 30. Hendrickje Stoffels, engaged as his housekeeper about 1649, eventually became his common-law wife and was the model for many of his pictures. Despite Rembrandt's financial success as an artist, teacher, and art dealer, his penchant for ostentatious living forced him to declare bankruptcy in 1656. An inventory of his collection of art and antiquities, taken before an auction to pay his debts, showed the breadth of Rembrandt's interests: ancient sculpture, Flemish and Italian Renaissance paintings, Far Eastern art, contemporary Dutch works, weapons, and armor. Unfortunately, the results of the auction - including the sale of his house - were disappointing.

These problems in no way affected Rembrandt's work; if anything, his artistry increased. Some of the great paintings from this period are The Jewish Bride (1665), The Syndics of the Cloth Guild (1661, Rijksmuseum, Amsterdam), Bathsheba (1654, Louvre, Paris), Jacob Blessing the Sons of Joseph (1656, Staatliche Gemäldegalerie, Kassel, Germany), and a self-portrait (1658, Frick Collection). His personal life, however, continued to be marred by sorrow. His beloved Hendrickje died in 1663, and his son, Titus, in 1668- only 27 years of age. Eleven months later, on October 4, 1669, Rembrandt died in Amsterdam.

Data source with acknowledgments - biography above extracted from: Web Gallery Of Art, http://www.wga.hu/index1

Joseph Mallord William Turner, better known as J.M.W. Turner, was born on April 23, 1775, in Covent Garden, London, England. A sickly child, Turner was sent to live with his uncle in rural England, and it was during this period that he began his artistic career. As a landscape painter, Turner brought luminosity and Romantic imagery to his subjects. His work—initially realistic—became more fluid and poetic, and is now regarded as a predecessor to Impressionism. Turner died on December 19, 1851, in Cheyne Walk, Chelsea, London, England.

Data source with acknowledgments Biography.com

The Author

Edward Lucie-Smith is an art critic and art historian, also a poet and photographer. He is generally regarded as the most prolific and widely published writer on contemporary art. Some of his books are used as standard texts throughout the world.

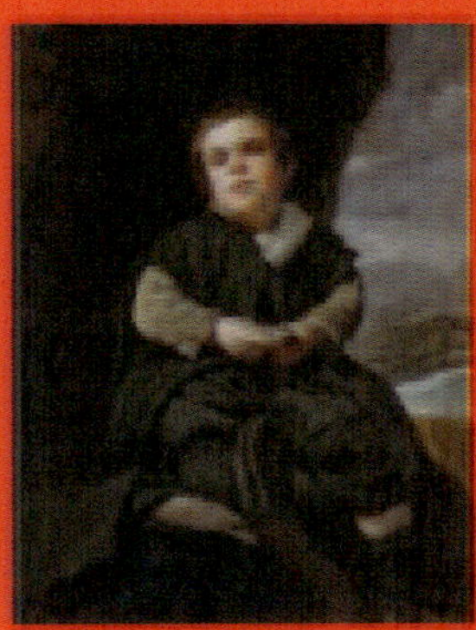
Edward Lucie-Smith
Uncollected Writings
Studies of Western Art
Cv/Visual Arts Research Series 152

Art . Travel . Histories

Published by Cv Publications
www.tracksdirectory.ision.co.uk

Printed in Dunstable, United Kingdom

85050666R00022